SUMMER CAMP

Every Summer
Has
It's Own Story

SUMMER CAMP

INCLUDED

- ↻ **Journal Entry Space for Three Camping Stays**
- ↻ **(2 weeks each)**
  Prompts Include:
- ↻ **Preparation**
- ↻ **1st Day Arrival**
- ↻ **14 days of special memories including:**
  - ↻ **weather**
  - ↻ **activities**
  - ↻ **feelings**
  - ↻ **friends**
  - ↻ **pictures (drawn or photos)**
- ↻ **Pages for 9 autographs per trip.**

PREPARATION

Packing (Things to remember):

	Year 1	Year 2	Year 3
CLOTHING			
Suitable clothing (include at least one warm sweater)	☐	☐	☐
Bathing suit	☐	☐	☐
Swim goggles	☐	☐	☐
Hat (with a brim)	☐	☐	☐
Rain Gear and/or Umbrella	☐	☐	☐
Rubber boots	☐	☐	☐
Flip Flops / Sandals	☐	☐	☐
Towels	☐	☐	☐
NECESSITIES			
Flashlight (w/batteries)	☐	☐	☐
Insect repellant	☐	☐	☐
Lip Balm	☐	☐	☐
Water Bottle	☐	☐	☐
Cell Phone/Camera – (w/charger)	☐	☐	☐
ENTERTAINMENT			
Favorite book(s)/ music	☐	☐	☐
Pencil Crayons	☐	☐	☐
Board games	☐	☐	☐
Supply of favorite snacks	☐	☐	☐

 PREPARATION

Important (Things to remember):

Contact Information - for parents or guardians
Alternative Contact Information
Medication — enough to cover the
        complete trip + a couple of extra days.

Important (Ensure that Camp Personnel know):

Allergies
Dietary Needs
Medical Conditions
Medications
Specifically where Parents will be
Specifically how Parents can be reached
Child's ability to swim

SUMMER CAMP

20 _____

START DATE _____

My name is _____ and this is the story of my stay at summer camp.   The camp is called _____. This is my (first) (_____) trip to this summer camp.

ARRIVAL

Arrived by:

When we arrived:

The first person I met was: _____ and this is what happened then:

My bunk mates are:

Our Counselor is: _____

Getting Settled

We are living in a:

After arriving at camp we:

_____
_____
_____
_____

The first meal that I had at camp was: - and it was.

_____
_____
_____
_____

How I felt at the end of the day:

_____
_____
_____
_____

SUMMER CAMP
DAY 1

_____day – the _____ of _____

The Weather -

Things we did today.

_____
_____
_____
_____
_____
_____
_____
_____
_____

Friends that I spent the day with.

_____
_____
_____

SUMMER CAMP
DAY 1

The best thing about today.

How I felt at the end of the day:

My picture memory for the day..

SUMMER CAMP

DAY 2

_____day – the _____ of _____

--- **Day** ------------ **Date** ----- **Month** ----

The Weather -

Things we did today.

_____
_____
_____
_____
_____
_____
_____
_____
_____
_____
_____

Friends that I spent the day with.

_____
_____
_____

SUMMER CAMP

 ## DAY 2

The best thing about today.

How I felt at the end of the day:

My picture memory for the day..

SUMMER CAMP

DAY 3

_____day – the _____ of _____

--- **Day** ------------ **Date** ----- **Month** ----

The Weather -

Things we did today.

Friends that I spent the day with.

SUMMER CAMP

DAY 3

The best thing about today.

How I felt at the end of the day:

My picture memory for the day..

SUMMER CAMP

DAY 4

_____day – the _____ of _____

--- Day ------------ Date ----- Month ----

The Weather -

Things we did today.

_____
_____
_____
_____
_____
_____
_____
_____

Friends that I spent the day with.

_____
_____
_____

SUMMER CAMP

DAY 4

The best thing about today.

How I felt at the end of the day:

My picture memory for the day..

SUMMER CAMP
DAY 5

_____day – the _____ of _____
--- Day ------------ Date ----- Month ----

The Weather -

Things we did today.

_____
_____
_____
_____
_____
_____
_____
_____
_____
_____

Friends that I spent the day with.

_____
_____
_____

SUMMER CAMP

 ## DAY 5

The best thing about today.

How I felt at the end of the day:

My picture memory for the day..

SUMMER CAMP
DAY 6

_____day – the _____ of _____

--- **Day** ------------ **Date** ----- **Month** ----

The Weather -

Things we did today.

_____

_____

_____

_____

_____

_____

_____

_____

Friends that I spent the day with.

_____

_____

_____

SUMMER CAMP

DAY 6

The best thing about today.

How I felt at the end of the day:

My picture memory for the day..

SUMMER CAMP

DAY 7

_____day – the _____ of _____
--- Day ------------ Date ----- Month ----

The Weather -

Things we did today.

Friends that I spent the day with.

SUMMER CAMP
DAY 7

The best thing about today.

How I felt at the end of the day:

My picture memory for the day..

SUMMER CAMP
DAY 8

_____day – the _____ of _____

--- Day ------------ Date ----- Month ----

The Weather -

Things we did today.

Friends that I spent the day with.

SUMMER CAMP
DAY 8

The best thing about today.

How I felt at the end of the day:

My picture memory for the day..

SUMMER CAMP

DAY 9

_____day – the _____ of _____

--- Day ------------ Date ----- Month ----

The Weather -

Things we did today.

_____
_____
_____
_____
_____
_____
_____
_____
_____

Friends that I spent the day with.

_____
_____
_____

SUMMER CAMP

DAY 9

The best thing about today.

How I felt at the end of the day:

My picture memory for the day..

SUMMER CAMP
DAY 10

_____day – the _____ of _____

--- Day ------------ Date ----- Month ----

The Weather -

Things we did today.

_____
_____
_____
_____
_____
_____
_____
_____
_____

Friends that I spent the day with.

_____
_____
_____

SUMMER CAMP
DAY 10

The best thing about today.

How I felt at the end of the day:

My picture memory for the day..

SUMMER CAMP
DAY 11

_____day – the _____ of _____

--- Day ------------ Date ----- Month ----

The Weather -

Things we did today.

_____

_____

_____

_____

_____

_____

_____

_____

Friends that I spent the day with.

_____

_____

_____

SUMMER CAMP
DAY 11

The best thing about today.

How I felt at the end of the day:

My picture memory for the day..

SUMMER CAMP
DAY 12

_____day – the _____ of _____

--- **Day** ------------ **Date** ----- **Month** ----

The Weather -

Things we did today.

_____
_____
_____
_____
_____
_____
_____
_____
_____
_____

Friends that I spent the day with.

_____
_____
_____

SUMMER CAMP
DAY 12

The best thing about today.

How I felt at the end of the day:

My picture memory for the day..

SUMMER CAMP
DAY 13

_____day – the _____ of _____

--- **Day** ------------ **Date** ----- **Month** ----

The Weather -

Things we did today.

_____
_____
_____
_____
_____
_____
_____
_____
_____

Friends that I spent the day with.

_____
_____
_____

SUMMER CAMP
DAY 13

The best thing about today.

How I felt at the end of the day:

My picture memory for the day..

SUMMER CAMP
LAST DAY

Special things we did today.

Friends that I spent the day with.

SUMMER CAMP
LAST DAY

The best thing about camp.

How I felt at the end of camp:

My best friend at camp was:

Something new that I learned at camp:

Something I want to do next year at camp:

SUMMER CAMP

AUTOGRAPHS

My Friend

Message

My Friend

Message

My Friend

Message

SUMMER CAMP

AUTOGRAPHS

My Friend

Message

My Friend

Message

My Friend

Message

SUMMER CAMP
AUTOGRAPHS

My Friend

Message

My Friend

Message

My Friend

Message

SUMMER CAMP

20 ____

START DATE _____

My name is _____ and this is the story of my summer camp.   The camp is called _____.   This is my (first) (_____) trip to this summer camp.

ARRIVAL

Arrived by:

When we arrived:

_____
_____
_____
_____

The first person I met was: _____ and this
is what happened then:

_____
_____
_____
_____

My bunk mates are:

_____
_____
_____
_____

Our Counselor is: _____

Getting Settled

We are living in a:

After arriving at camp we:

The first meal that I had at camp was: - and it was.

How I felt at the end of the day:

SUMMER CAMP
DAY 1

_____day – the _____ of _____

--- **Day** ------------ **Date** ----- **Month** ----

The Weather -

Things we did today.

Friends that I spent the day with.

SUMMER CAMP
DAY 1

The best thing about today.

How I felt at the end of the day:

My picture memory for the day..

SUMMER CAMP
DAY 2

_____day – the _____ of _____

--- Day ------------ Date ----- Month ----

The Weather -

Things we did today.

Friends that I spent the day with.

SUMMER CAMP
DAY 2

The best thing about today.

How I felt at the end of the day:

My picture memory for the day..

SUMMER CAMP
DAY 3

_____day – the _____ of _____
--- **Day** ------------ **Date** ----- **Month** ----

The Weather -

Things we did today.

_____
_____
_____
_____
_____
_____
_____
_____
_____
_____

Friends that I spent the day with.

_____
_____
_____

SUMMER CAMP
DAY 3

The best thing about today.

How I felt at the end of the day:

My picture memory for the day..

SUMMER CAMP
DAY 4

_____day – the _____ of _____
--- **Day** ------------ **Date** ----- **Month** ----

The Weather -

Things we did today.

Friends that I spent the day with.

SUMMER CAMP
DAY 4

The best thing about today.

How I felt at the end of the day:

My picture memory for the day..

SUMMER CAMP
DAY 5

_____day – the _____ of _____

--- **Day** ------------ **Date** ----- **Month** ----

The Weather -

Things we did today.

_____
_____
_____
_____
_____
_____
_____
_____

Friends that I spent the day with.

_____
_____
_____

SUMMER CAMP
DAY 5

The best thing about today.

How I felt at the end of the day:

My picture memory for the day..

SUMMER CAMP
DAY 6

_____day – the _____ of _____

--- **Day** ------------ **Date** ----- **Month** ----

The Weather -

Things we did today.

_____
_____
_____
_____
_____
_____
_____
_____
_____

Friends that I spent the day with.

_____
_____
_____

SUMMER CAMP
DAY 6

The best thing about today.

How I felt at the end of the day:

My picture memory for the day..

SUMMER CAMP
DAY 7

_____day – the _____ of _____

--- **Day** ------------ **Date** ----- **Month** ----

The Weather -

Things we did today.

_____
_____
_____
_____
_____
_____
_____
_____
_____

Friends that I spent the day with.

_____
_____
_____

SUMMER CAMP
DAY 7

The best thing about today.

How I felt at the end of the day:

My picture memory for the day..

SUMMER CAMP
DAY 8

_____day – the _____ of _____

--- **Day** ------------ **Date** ----- **Month** ----

The Weather -

Things we did today.

Friends that I spent the day with.

SUMMER CAMP
DAY 8

The best thing about today.

How I felt at the end of the day:

My picture memory for the day..

SUMMER CAMP
DAY 9

_____day – the _____ of _____

--- **Day** ------------ **Date** ----- **Month** ----

The Weather -

Things we did today.

Friends that I spent the day with.

SUMMER CAMP
DAY 9

The best thing about today.

How I felt at the end of the day:

My picture memory for the day..

SUMMER CAMP
DAY 10

_____day – the _____ of _____

--- Day ------------ Date ----- Month ----

The Weather -

Things we did today.

_____
_____
_____
_____
_____
_____
_____
_____
_____

Friends that I spent the day with.

_____
_____
_____

SUMMER CAMP
DAY 10

The best thing about today.

How I felt at the end of the day:

My picture memory for the day..

SUMMER CAMP
DAY 11

_____day – the _____ of _____
--- **Day** ------------ **Date** ----- **Month** ----

The Weather -

Things we did today.

_____
_____
_____
_____
_____
_____
_____
_____
_____

Friends that I spent the day with.

_____
_____
_____

SUMMER CAMP
DAY 11

The best thing about today.

How I felt at the end of the day:

My picture memory for the day..

SUMMER CAMP
DAY 12

_____day – the _____ of _____

--- **Day** ------------ **Date** ----- **Month** ----

The Weather -

Things we did today.

Friends that I spent the day with.

SUMMER CAMP
DAY 12

The best thing about today.

How I felt at the end of the day:

My picture memory for the day..

SUMMER CAMP
DAY 13

_____day – the _____ of _____
--- **Day** ------------ **Date** ----- **Month** ----

The Weather -

Things we did today.

_____
_____
_____
_____
_____
_____
_____
_____
_____
_____

Friends that I spent the day with.

_____
_____
_____

SUMMER CAMP
DAY 13

The best thing about today.

How I felt at the end of the day:

My picture memory for the day..

SUMMER CAMP

LAST DAY

Special things we did today.

_____
_____
_____
_____
_____
_____
_____
_____
_____

Friends that I spent the day with.

_____
_____
_____

_____
_____
_____

SUMMER CAMP
LAST DAY

The best thing about camp.

How I felt at the end of camp:

My best friend at camp was:

Something new that I learned at camp:

Something I want to do next year at camp:

SUMMER CAMP

AUTOGRAPHS

My Friend

Message

My Friend

Message

My Friend

Message

SUMMER CAMP

AUTOGRAPHS

My Friend

Message

My Friend

Message

My Friend

Message

SUMMER CAMP

AUTOGRAPHS

My Friend

Message

My Friend

Message

My Friend

Message

SUMMER CAMP
20 _____

START DATE _____

My name is _____ and this is the story of my summer camp. The camp is called _____. This is my (first) (_____) trip to this summer camp.

ARRIVAL

Arrived by:

When we arrived:

_____
_____
_____
_____

The first person I met was: _____ and this
is what happened then:

_____
_____
_____
_____

My bunk mates are:

_____
_____
_____
_____

Our Counselor is: _____

Getting Settled

We are living in a:

After arriving at camp we:

The first meal that I had at camp was: - and it was.

How I felt at the end of the day:

SUMMER CAMP
DAY 1

_____day – the _____ of _____

--- **Day** ------------ **Date** ----- **Month** ----

The Weather -

Things we did today.

Friends that I spent the day with.

SUMMER CAMP
DAY 1

The best thing about today.

How I felt at the end of the day:

My picture memory for the day..

SUMMER CAMP
DAY 2

_____day – the _____ of _____

--- **Day** ------------ **Date** ----- **Month** ----

The Weather -

Things we did today.

_____
_____
_____
_____
_____
_____
_____
_____
_____
_____

Friends that I spent the day with.

_____
_____
_____

SUMMER CAMP
DAY 2

The best thing about today.

How I felt at the end of the day:

My picture memory for the day..

SUMMER CAMP
DAY 3

_____day – the _____ of _____

--- **Day** ------------ **Date** ----- **Month** ----

The Weather -

Things we did today.

_____
_____
_____
_____
_____
_____
_____
_____

Friends that I spent the day with.

_____
_____
_____

SUMMER CAMP
DAY 3

The best thing about today.

How I felt at the end of the day:

My picture memory for the day..

SUMMER CAMP
DAY 4

_____day – the _____ of _____
--- **Day** ------------ **Date** ----- **Month** ----

The Weather -

Things we did today.

Friends that I spent the day with.

SUMMER CAMP
DAY 4

The best thing about today.

How I felt at the end of the day:

My picture memory for the day..

SUMMER CAMP
DAY 5

_____day – the _____ of _____

--- **Day** ------------ **Date** ----- **Month** ----

The Weather -

Things we did today.

Friends that I spent the day with.

SUMMER CAMP
DAY 5

The best thing about today.

How I felt at the end of the day:

My picture memory for the day..

SUMMER CAMP
DAY 6

_____day – the _____ of _____

--- **Day** ------------ **Date** ----- **Month** ----

The Weather -

Things we did today.

Friends that I spent the day with.

SUMMER CAMP
DAY 6

The best thing about today.

How I felt at the end of the day:

My picture memory for the day..

SUMMER CAMP
DAY 7

_____day – the _____ of _____

--- **Day** ------------ **Date** ----- **Month** ----

The Weather -

Things we did today.

_____
_____
_____
_____
_____
_____
_____
_____
_____

Friends that I spent the day with.

_____
_____
_____

SUMMER CAMP
DAY 7

The best thing about today.

_____
_____
_____

How I felt at the end of the day: 😦 😠 😟 😀

My picture memory for the day..

SUMMER CAMP
DAY 8

_____day – the _____ of _____

--- Day ------------ Date ----- Month ----

The Weather -

Things we did today.

_____
_____
_____
_____
_____
_____
_____
_____
_____
_____
_____

Friends that I spent the day with.

_____
_____
_____

SUMMER CAMP
DAY 8

The best thing about today.

How I felt at the end of the day:

My picture memory for the day..

SUMMER CAMP
DAY 9

_____day – the _____ of _____

--- **Day** ------------- **Date** ----- **Month** ----

The Weather -

Things we did today.

Friends that I spent the day with.

SUMMER CAMP
DAY 9

The best thing about today.

How I felt at the end of the day:

My picture memory for the day..

SUMMER CAMP
DAY 10

_____day – the _____ of _____
--- **Day** ----
Month :

The Weather -

Things we did today.

Friends that I spent the day with.

SUMMER CAMP
DAY 10

The best thing about today.

How I felt at the end of the day:

My picture memory for the day..

SUMMER CAMP
DAY 11

_____day – the _____ of _____

--- **Day** ------------ **Date** ----- **Month** ----

The Weather -

Things we did today.

Friends that I spent the day with.

SUMMER CAMP
DAY 11

The best thing about today.

How I felt at the end of the day:

My picture memory for the day..

SUMMER CAMP
DAY 12

_____day – the _____ of _____
--- Day ------------ Date ----- Month ----

The Weather -

Things we did today.

_____
_____
_____
_____
_____
_____
_____
_____
_____
_____

Friends that I spent the day with.

_____
_____
_____

SUMMER CAMP
DAY 12

The best thing about today.

How I felt at the end of the day:

My picture memory for the day..

SUMMER CAMP
DAY 13

_____day – the _____ of _____

--- **Day** ------------ **Date** ----- **Month** ----

The Weather -

Things we did today.

_____
_____
_____
_____
_____
_____
_____
_____

Friends that I spent the day with.

_____
_____
_____

SUMMER CAMP
DAY 13

The best thing about today.

How I felt at the end of the day:

My picture memory for the day..

SUMMER CAMP
LAST DAY

Special things we did today.

Friends that I spent the day with.

SUMMER CAMP
LAST DAY

The best thing about camp.

How I felt at the end of camp:

My best friend at camp was:

Something new that I learned at camp:

Something I want to do next year at camp:

SUMMER CAMP
AUTOGRAPHS

My Friend

Message

My Friend

Message

My Friend

Message

SUMMER CAMP
AUTOGRAPHS

My Friend

Message

My Friend

Message

My Friend

Message

SUMMER CAMP
AUTOGRAPHS

My Friend

Message

My Friend

Message

My Friend

Message

MEMORIES

MEMORIES

MEMORIES

MEMORIES

MEMORIES

MEMORIES

MEMORIES

MEMORIES

MEMORIES

MEMORIES

MEMORIES

Made in United States
North Haven, CT
23 June 2023